TREETOPS

Stage 15
Teaching Notes

Jo Tregenza

Contents

Introduction	4
Comprehension strategies	6
Links to other TreeTops titles	7
Curriculum coverage chart	8

Black Beauty

Synopsis	11
Group or guided reading	12
Speaking, listening and drama activities	14
Writing activities	14

20,000 Leagues Under the Sea

Synopsis	16
Group or guided reading	17
Speaking, listening and drama activities	19
Writing activities	19

Gulliver's Travels

Synopsis	21
Group or guided reading	22
Speaking, listening and drama activities	24
Writing activities	24

The Lost World

Synopsis	26
Group or guided reading	27
Speaking, listening and drama activities	29
Writing activities	29

David Copperfield

Synopsis	31
Group or guided reading	32
Speaking, listening and drama activities	34
Writing activities	34

Moonfleet

Synopsis	36
Group or guided reading	37
Speaking, listening and drama activities	39
Writing activities	39

Introduction

TreeTops Classics are abridged versions of classic texts especially chosen to appeal to 9- to 11-year-olds. They are ideal for use in group sessions and as model texts for writing. They are also an excellent stimulus for other writing activities and for speaking, listening and drama.

TreeTops Stages follow on from the Oxford Reading Tree Stages and are designed to be used flexibly, matched to individual pupils' reading ability.

How to introduce the books

Before reading the book, read the title and the blurb on the back cover. Ask the children what they think will happen. Read both authors' names (original author and abridger) and talk about books by the same authors that the children may have read or heard of. Look through the book briefly to find pictures of the main characters and discover the setting for the story.

Complete the reading session with the pupils telling you what they enjoyed about the story, encouraging them to refer to the text to support their reasons.

Using this Teaching Notes booklet

These Teaching Notes provide guidance for using the book with groups of pupils or with individuals. Suggestions are provided for group and guided reading, speaking, listening and drama, writing and cross-curricular links. The activities largely focus on strategies to increase comprehension (see the comprehension strategies grid on page 6) and include vocabulary development activities (a key part of improving comprehension).

In order to support your planning and record keeping, the curriculum coverage chart on pages 8–10 provides curriculum information relating to the curricula for England, Wales, Northern Ireland and Scotland. This includes PNS Literacy Framework objectives, Assessment Focuses and the reading, writing and speaking and listening levels children can reasonably be expected to be achieving when reading these TreeTops books.

Notes for adults and children in TreeTops Classics books

Included on the inside covers are notes to help parents/carers or classroom assistants share the books with children and questions to ask to help improve comprehension. (Answers to these are on the inside back cover of the books.) For children to read themselves there are:

- biographies of the original authors
- biographies of the abridging authors
- historical background information to help them understand the context of the story
- footnotes to explain difficult or archaic vocabulary.

Comprehension strategies

Book Title	Comprehension strategy taught through these Teaching Notes					
	Predicting	Questioning	Clarifying	Summarising	Imagining	Deducing
Black Beauty	✓	✓	✓	✓	✓	✓
20,000 Leagues Under the Sea	✓	✓	✓	✓	✓	✓
Gulliver's Travels	✓	✓	✓	✓	✓	✓
The Lost World	✓	✓	✓	✓	✓	✓
David Copperfield	✓	✓	✓	✓	✓	✓
Moonfleet	✓	✓	✓	✓	✓	✓

Links to other treetops titles

TreeTops Classics Stage 15	Range	Other TreeTops Classics titles with similar ranges
Black Beauty	Classic animal story	White Fang (Stage 14) The Jungle Book (Stage 14)
20,000 Leagues Under the Sea	Classic science fiction story	The Lost World (Stage 15) Dr Jekyll and Mr Hyde (Stage 16) Frankenstein (Stage 16)
Gulliver's Travels	Classic fantasy story	Five Children and It (Stage 14)
The Lost World	Classic science fiction story	20,000 Leagues Under the Sea (Stage 15) Frankenstein (Stage 16) Dr Jekyll and Mr Hyde (Stage 16)
David Copperfield	Classic realistic story	The Secret Garden (Stage 14) Jane Eyre (Stage 16) Oliver Twist (Stage 16) Wuthering Heights (Stage 16)
Moonfleet	Classic adventure story	The Three Musketeers (Stage 14) Kidnapped (Stage 16) Robinson Crusoe (Stage 16) Treasure Island (Stage 16)

Curriculum coverage chart

	Speaking, listening, drama	Reading	Writing
Black Beauty			
PNS Literacy Framework (Y6)	1.2	**V C** 7.2	9.4
National Curriculum (Y6)	Level 4/5	Level 4/5 AF 2, 3, 5	Level 4/5 AF 2
Scotland (5–14) (P7)	Level D, E	Level D, E	Level D, E
N. Ireland (P7/Y7)	1, 3, 4, 5, 9, 10	1, 2, 3, 4, 6, 9	1, 4, 6, 7
Wales (Y6)	Range: 1, 3, 4, 5 Skills: 1, 4, 5, 6, 7 Language & Development: 1, 4	R: 1, 2, 3, 5, 6 S: 1, 3, 4, 7 L & D: 1	R: 1, 4, 5 S: 4, 5 L & D: 4, 5
20,000 Leagues Under the Sea			
PNS Literacy Framework (Y6)	1.3	**V C** 7.2	9.1
National Curriculum (Y6)	Level 4/5	Level 4/5 AF 2, 3, 7	Level 4/5 AF 2, 3
Scotland (5–14) (P7)	Level D, E	Level D, E	Level D, E
N. Ireland (P7/Y7)	1, 3, 4, 5, 11	1, 2, 3, 4, 6, 9, 10	1, 4, 6, 7
Wales (Y6)	Range: 1, 3, 4 Skills: 1, 4, 5, 6, 7 Language & Development: 1, 4	R: 1, 2, 3, 5, 6 S: 1, 3, 7	R: 1, 3, 4, 5 S: 1, 2, 4 L & D: 4

C = Language comprehension   **V** = Vocabulary enrichment
AF = Assessment Focus   Y = Year   P = Primary

Curriculum coverage chart

	Speaking, listening, drama	Reading	Writing
Gulliver's Travels			
PNS Literacy Framework (Y6)	1.1	**V C** 7.2	10.2
National Curriculum (Y6)	Level 4/5	Level 4/5 AF 3, 6, 7	Level 4/5 AF 3, 4
Scotland (5–14) (P7)	Level D, E	Level D, E	Level D, E
N. Ireland (P7/Y7)	1, 3, 4, 5, 9, 11	1, 2, 3, 4, 6, 7, 9	1, 4
Wales (Y6)	Range: 1, 3, 4, 5 Skills: 1, 4, 5, 6, 7 Language & Development: 1, 4	R: 1, 2, 3, 5, 6 S: 1, 3, 4, 7 L & D: 1	R: 1, 3, 4, 5 S: 1, 4 L & D: 4
The Lost World			
PNS Literacy Framework (Y6)	1.1	**C** 7.3	9.3
National Curriculum (Y6)	Level 4/5	Level 4/5 AF 2, 3, 5, 6	Level 4/5 AF 2
Scotland (5–14) (P7)	Level D, E	Level D, E	Level D, E
N. Ireland (P7/Y7)	1, 5, 9, 10, 13	1, 2, 3, 4, 6, 7, 9	1, 2, 4, 6
Wales (Y6)	Range: 1, 2, 3, 4, 5 Skills: 1, 2, 4, 5, 6, 7 Language & Development: 1, 4	R: 1, 2, 3, 5, 6 S: 1, 3, 4, 7 L & D: 1	R: 1, 2, 3, 4, 5 S: 1, 2, 4, 8 L & D: 4

C = Language comprehension   **V** = Vocabulary enrichment

AF = Assessment Focus   Y = Year   P = Primary

Curriculum coverage chart

	Speaking, listening, drama	Reading	Writing
David Copperfield			
PNS Literacy Framework (Y6)	1.3	**V C** 8.2	9.4
National Curriculum (Y6)	Level 4/5	Level 4/5 AF 2, 3, 7	Level 4/5 AF 1, 7
Scotland (5–14) (P7)	Level D, E	Level D, E	Level D, E
N. Ireland (P7/Y7)	1, 9, 10	1, 2, 3, 4, 6, 7, 9	1, 2, 3, 4, 6, 7
Wales (Y6)	Range: 1, 2, 3 Skills: 1, 2, 4, 5 Language & Development: 1, 4	R: 1, 2, 3, 5, 6 S: 1, 3, 4, 7 L & D: 1	R: 1, 2, 3, 4, 5 S: 1, 2, 4, 8 L & D: 4
Moonfleet			
PNS Literacy Framework (Y6)	4.3	**V C** 8.2	9.4
National Curriculum (Y6)	Level 4/5	Level 4/5 AF 2, 3, 5	Level 4/5 AF 1
Scotland (5–14) (P7)	Level D, E	Level D, E	Level D, E
N. Ireland (P7/Y7)	1, 2, 7, 8, 9, 13	1, 2, 3, 4, 6, 7, 9	1, 2, 3, 4, 6, 7
Wales (Y6)	Range: 1, 2, 5, 6 Skills: 1, 2 Language & Development: 4	R: 1, 2, 3, 5, 6 S: 1, 3, 4, 7 L & D: 1, 2	R: 1, 3, 4, 5 S: 2, 4, 8 L & D: 1, 2

C = Language comprehension   **V** = Vocabulary enrichment
AF = Assessment Focus   Y = Year   P = Primary

Black Beauty

Author: Anna Sewell (1820–1878)

Synopsis: *Black Beauty* is the autobiography of a horse, the 'Black Beauty' of the title, who narrates his own story. Having various owners who ask different tasks of him, Black Beauty grows and has numerous adventures. He starts as a riding horse, then a carriage horse, then a mistreated town cab horse before finding eventual happiness in a secure home. Through it all, Black Beauty finds strength and keeps a good temper despite his suffering.

Social and historical context: The book deals with the issue of the humane treatment of animals. *Black Beauty* also addresses several other social issues. It is set against a Victorian backdrop and shows the differences between the lives of the rich and poor. The character of Jerry Barker, the kind London cab driver, has to give up work when he develops bronchitis. This threatens to send his entire family into poverty. However, the kindness he has always shown to others is rewarded when a wealthy customer finds him alternative employment. Black Beauty's good character is also rewarded when he eventually finds a happy home.

C = Language comprehension **R, AF** = Reading Assessment Focus
V = Vocabulary enrichment **W, AF** = Writing Assessment Focus

Group or guided reading

Introducing the book

(C) *(Predicting)* Have the children heard of *Black Beauty*? What do they know already about the story? Provide a bag (ideally linked to the horse theme, e.g. a nosebag). The bag should contain some of the following items: horse rosette, horse whip (bamboo stick), smoking pipe, scarf, straw/hay, an item linked to London such as a toy red bus. Talk to the children about how these items are all linked to the story. Ask them to speculate about possible connections.

Assessment *(R, AF2)* Can the children use contextual clues to preview the story?

During reading

(C) *(Imagining)* Read the first chapter to the children and talk about any associations that come to your mind. Don't take oral contributions from the children – you want them to concentrate on building images in their head. Ask the children to picture the story as you read. Pause at key points and ask them to look at the picture in their head. Then ask them to give details beyond the direct information you have given them. For example, ask: *Why did Black Beauty think it served the man right that he had broken his neck?*

● *(Deducing)* Read Chapter 2 together. Can the children deduce the underlying theme that the author is trying to present? (That nurturing and caring for animals will reap rewards.)

Independent reading

(C) *(Deducing)* Ask the children to read Chapters 3–4. As they are reading, ask them to deduce information about the character of Black Beauty. Ask them to back up their opinions with direct references from the text.

Black Beauty

C *(Clarifying)* Focus on the style of writing. How is the text written? Can the children identify that it is written in the style of an autobiography?

Assessment Check that children:

- *(R, AF3)* can deduce information about the character of Black Beauty
- *(R, AF5)* can identify and describe some characteristics of the style of the writer.
- Ask the children to finish reading to the end of the story independently.

Returning and responding to the text

Objective Understand underlying themes, causes and points of view (7.2).

C *(Summarising)* Having read the story, ask the children to create a grid that will enable them to compare and contrast the different homes and jobs that Black Beauty had. Encourage them to think from both the horse's and the owners' point of view.

C *(Questioning)* Give the children sticky notes. As you read together, ask them to write questions that they would like to ask the owners of Black Beauty.

C *(Summarising, Clarifying)* Create an emotions grid to track the feelings of Black Beauty through the story. Add a range of emotions on the Y-axis ranging from the worst to the best, then put the chapters along the X-axis. Plot Black Beauty's emotions.

Assessment *(R, AF2)* Can the children sum up key ideas using evidence from the text?

Speaking, listening and drama activities

Objective Participate in whole-class debate using the conventions and language of debate (1.2).

- *(Questioning)* Ask the children to take on the role of some of the different owners of Black Beauty. Appoint a chairperson or judge to organise the debate. You might like to carry out the debate as if in a court of law, perhaps with one of the owners facing charges for neglect. Ask the children to carry out the debate by bringing forward other owners for witnesses.

Writing activities

Objective Select words and language drawing on their knowledge of literary features and formal and informal writing (9.4).

- **V** Use highlighter pens on sections of the text to identify language and/or technical vocabulary that is related to the specific time period.

- *(Questioning)* Go into role as a different owner of Black Beauty. Invite the children to interview the owner and discover whether they are kind or heartless.

- Having identified the personality of the owner, ask the children to write a new chapter about this owner in the style of the author (from Black Beauty's viewpoint).

Assessment *(W, AF2)* Has the style been adopted confidently?

Whole class reads
Books on a similar theme:

- *Watership Down* by Richard Adams
- *Tarka the Otter* by Henry Williamson
- *Born Free* by Joy Adamson

Cross-curricular links
History
- Children could compare the lives of the rich and poor in Victorian times.

Geography
- Compare Black Beauty's country life with city life. Describe and explain how and why urban places are both similar to and different from rural places in the same country.

20,000 Leagues Under the Sea

Author: Jules Verne (1828–1905)

Synopsis: The story tells of the adventures of three men – a naturalist, his colleague and a whale-hunter – as they explore beneath the sea while they are held captive by Captain Nemo, in his submarine Nautilus. They adventure across the world beneath the oceans meeting many challenges – huge icebergs, angry sharks and terrifying squids. They survive them all until one day Nemo's submarine meets a huge maelstrom and the three men make their bid for freedom.

Social and historical context: The book is based at the end of the nineteenth century at a time when many explorers were discovering new species and ideas. Charles Darwin had published his book *On the Origin of Species*. It was also a time when advances in science and technology inspired the writing of popular science fiction novels. This book features a large submarine at the time when this kind of technology was only just emerging. The book also raises the issue of animal rights, as it challenges readers to consider whether or not whale hunting should be carried out.

C = Language comprehension   **R, AF** = Reading Assessment Focus
V = Vocabulary enrichment   **W, AF** = Writing Assessment Focus

Group or guided reading

Introducing the book

(C) *(Predicting)* Ask the children whether they know what the title means. Have they ever heard of 'leagues' in this context? Explain that leagues are an old-fashioned measurement of distance. In the book the characters travel a very long distance. The title means they travel 20,000 leagues in distance – not 20,000 leagues in depth. Ask the children: *Look at the front cover. What might happen in this story?*

During reading

(C) *(Imagining)* Read up to page 15. Ask the children to draw a picture of what they imagine the *Abraham Lincoln* ship to look like based on the description.

(V) Find any vocabulary in the text that relates to the ship and label these on the picture. Encourage children to find other vocabulary that describes items on a ship and label these.

(C) *(Predicting, Imagining)* Now re-read this section focusing on the description of the sea monster. Ask the children to draw what they think it might look like.

(C) *(Deducing)* Now read to the end of the chapter with the children, but as you are reading, ask them to tell you when they think they know what the monster is.

Assessment *(R, AF3)* Can children use clues from the text to draw conclusions?

Independent reading

C *(Clarifying, Summarising, Deducing)* Ask the children to read Chapters 3–6. As they read, explain to them that you would like them to create character profiles for the four main characters: Pierre Aronnax, Conseil, Ned Land and Captain Nemo. These chapters give several clues about the personalities of each.

Assessment Check that children:

- *(R, AF2)* can retrieve key information about the characters

- *(R, AF7)* understand how the elements of the story are related to the historical period.

- Ask the children to finish reading to the end of the story independently.

Returning and responding to the text

Objective Understand underlying themes, causes and points of view (7.2).

C *(Questioning)* What questions would the children like to ask Captain Nemo? There are two main questions threaded through the story: *Why is Nemo sailing the seas? What has happened to make him so angry?*

C *(Clarifying)* Ask children to consider the date 1867, when the submarine is prowling the waters. Perhaps there is a significant event in history that could have led to Captain Nemo's anger? Ask the children to use the internet or books to do research and see if they can come up with some possible suggestions.

Assessment *(R, AF3)* Can the children infer and interpret key ideas using evidence from the text?

Speaking, listening and drama activities

Objective Use the techniques of dialogic talk to explore, ideas, topics or issues (1.3).

- *(Questioning, Clarifying)* Ask the children to carry out a group discussion to consider the issues in Chapter 4. In the chapter, Ned (a whale hunter) becomes angry at how Captain Nemo slaughters the orcas. Ask: *Why is Ned angry when he himself is a whale hunter?* Encourage children to take on different roles in the discussion, e.g. spokesperson, protagonist, questioner.

Writing activities

Objective Set their own challenges to extend achievement and experiences in writing (9.1).

- *(Imagining, Clarifying)* Give children the option to write one of the following: an additional chapter to the story written in the style of the author that either reveals why Captain Nemo is sailing the seas or explains what has happened to his family; a discursive piece about whether the orcas should have been slaughtered.

Assessment *(W, AF2)* Are the main style features clear? Is the purpose of the writing maintained?

- *(W, AF3)* Is the text presented and sequenced effectively? Are the views consistent throughout?

Whole class reads
Books on a similar theme:
- *Journey to the Centre of the Earth* by Jules Verne
- *Kensuke's Kingdom* by Michael Morpurgo
- *Stormsearch* by Robert Westall

Cross-curricular links
Geography
- Children can map the journey of the submarine.

Science/ Design & Technology
- Engage the children in designing a submarine that can float and sink.

I.C.T.
- Use 'Google Earth' or a similar software program to view the places that the submarine visits.

Gulliver's Travels

Author: Jonathan Swift (1667–1745)

Synopsis: Lemuel Gulliver is a traveller who sails to many strange lands. After a shipwreck, he lands in Lilliput. After being captured he is guaranteed freedom if he helps the Lilliputians to fight the Blefuscans. Next, he visits Brobdingnag, a land of giants. He is kept in a little box and looked after by a farmer's daughter, Glumdalclitch. The king of Brobdingnag, after learning about Gulliver's country, concludes that humans are very unpleasant. Other adventures include meeting the Laputans on a flying island and encountering a race of dignified horses, called Houyhnhnms, who make Gulliver rethink his feelings towards humans. He eventually returns home, spending most of his time with his horses.

Social and historical context: Through devising many different lands and societies, Jonathan Swift holds up a satirical mirror to the European way of life in the early eighteenth century. On his travels Gulliver encounters extremes such as petty politics and violent warfare, as well as alternatives such as peaceful societies with little need for laws to regulate behaviour. The book challenges readers' assumptions of what is right and wrong, as we see Gulliver learn important lessons from each place that he visits.

- **C** = Language comprehension
- **V** = Vocabulary enrichment
- **R, AF** = Reading Assessment Focus
- **W, AF** = Writing Assessment Focus

Group or guided reading

Introducing the book

(C) *(Predicting, Questioning)* Discuss the front cover. What do children think is going on in the picture? Model some questions to think about such as: *Why do you think that the large person is being held down? Is he a giant or are the smaller people particularly small?* What questions can the children generate from the front cover? Look at the list of chapter titles. What conclusions can the children draw about the story?

During reading

- Prior to the guided reading session ask the children to read Chapters 1–3 independently.

(C) *(Clarifying, Summarising)* Ask the children what they have understood of the story so far. What do they feel about Gulliver and the Lilliputians?

(C) *(Clarifying)* Read Chapters 4–6 with the children. Discuss how the author has forced the reader to see the story from a different point of view by reversing the scenario and making Gulliver the tiny person in a giant land.

(V) Ask the children to gather vocabulary relating to the emotions and responses of the characters, e.g. 'overjoyed' on page 31. It would be helpful to have a picture of Gulliver and one of a giant, e.g. Glumdalclitch. Children can then arrange their chosen words around those pictures. Encourage children to add more descriptive words using a thesaurus.

Independent reading

C *(Imagining)* Ask the children to read to the end of the book. As they are reading ask them to try to plot a map of Gulliver's journey across the world. Encourage them to consider how the other people that he meets feel about Gulliver.

Assessment Check that children:

- *(R, AF3)* can identify the relationships between the characters
- *(R, AF6)* can consider different points of view about the main character.

Returning and responding to the text

Objective Understand underlying themes, causes and points of view (7.2).

C *(Deducing)* Having read the whole book, discuss with the children what the main issues of the story might be. Can they pick out the key themes? Do they understand how the author has tried to poke fun at the systems that exist in England? Can they draw conclusions about the author's beliefs about war? Ask the children to consider why this book may have been particularly influential.

Assessment *(R, AF6)* Can the children identify and comment on the writer's purpose and viewpoint?

- *(R, AF7)* Can the children relate the text to its social and historical background? Can they explain why the story might have been influential?

Speaking, listening and drama activities

Objective Use a range of oral techniques to present persuasive arguments and engaging narratives (1.1).

- *(Imagining, Questioning)* Imagine that Gulliver decided to stay and stand trial in Lilliput. Ask the children to take on different roles and carry out the court case for Gulliver. Emphasise the importance of children stating their point of view clearly and considering their audience. Encourage the rest of the group to ask appropriate questions to elicit the information they need to make a decision about the case.

Writing activities

Objective Use paragraphs to achieve pace and emphasis (10.2).

- Re-read pages 41–44. Discuss the different inventions with the children.
- Invite the children to work with a partner to discuss different ideas for zany inventions that could never work.
- Ask them to write an explanation for their crazy invention including an introductory paragraph and a conclusion.

Assessment *(W, AF3, AF4)* Can the children organise ideas in a sequence of paragraphs, and include an introduction matched to purpose and a fitting conclusion?

Whole class reads

Books on a similar theme:

- *The Poppykettle Papers* by Robert Ingpen and Michael Lawrence
- *The Selfish Giant* by Oscar Wilde
- *The Iron Man* by Ted Hughes

Cross-curricular links

Geography
- Make maps of Gulliver's journeys.

Design & Technology
- Create a home for Gulliver in a shoebox.

History
- Undertake a class project on 18th century Britain. Different groups could be assigned a key topic such as government, laws, clothing, family life, and so on.

The Lost World

Author: Arthur Conan Doyle (1859–1930)

Synopsis: Lost worlds, dinosaurs, explorers and ape-men are all ingredients of this story. It tells the tale of four explorers each with very different characteristics and a different reason for their journey. The eccentric and passionate Professor Challenger tells an audience all about the 'Lost World' that he has discovered. As he has no proof other than a dubious photograph, no one believes him. He sets the challenge for a team to go and visit it for themselves. He is joined by eager young reporter Ed Malone, academic rival and sceptic Professor Summerlee, and the adventurous explorer Lord Roxton. The four men set off and soon discover a hidden world with many adventures.

Social and historical context: This story is set in Edwardian England at a time when exploring was very much in vogue. Published in 1912, it was the era of daring arctic explorers such as Shackleton and Scott. The author portrays men who are courageous, forthright and loyal, perhaps setting an example for young readers of the time on how they should grow up to behave.

C = Language comprehension   *R, AF* = Reading Assessment Focus
V = Vocabulary enrichment   *W, AF* = Writing Assessment Focus

Group or guided reading

Introducing the book

(C) *(Predicting, Deducing)* Look at the front cover. Do children know what the animal is? Can they make a prediction about what the Lost World might be? Look at the chapter headings on the contents page. Ask the children: *What can you infer from these headings?*

During reading

(C) *(Deducing)* Before reading, prepare a chart with the names of the four main characters on it. As you read Chapters 1–3, ask the children to make notes on the chart of any clues about the characteristics of the four main characters. Ask them to consider how these people interact. Why do they think the author chose these characteristics? Draw attention to the way the author implies characteristics through actions.

Objective Understand how writers create impact (7.3).

(C) *(Clarifying)* Focus on the language and style the author uses. Draw children's attention to the use of dialogue to open the story. Why has the author chosen to do this?

- Focus on the way that the author has described characters. Do the children notice how the author uses animal characteristics to describe people?

Assessment *(R, AF5)* Can the children identify how the writer uses actions to imply characteristics?

The Lost World

Independent reading

C *(Summarising)* Ask the children to read Chapters 5–7. Give them small writing pads to use as reporter's notebooks. Ask them to take notes as they read that could be used to write a news report on these chapters. When they have finished reading, ask them to use their notes to summarise the story.

Assessment Check that children:

- *(R, AF2)* can summarise the main parts of the story
- *(R, AF3)* can identify the relationships between the characters.
- Ask the children to finish reading to the end of the story independently.

Returning and responding to the text

C *(Imagining)* Re-read Chapter 6. Challenge the children to create a map of the Lost World.

C *(Imagining, Questioning)* Ask the children to imagine that they are in the audience when the explorers return. Ask: *What questions would you ask them?*

C *(Deducing)* Can the children consider the story from a different point of view? Ask: *What if the story had been written by Professor Challenger? How would the story be different?* Children might like to hot seat the professor to explore his point of view.

Assessment Check that children:

- *(R, AF2)* can retrieve information from the text
- *(R, AF6)* can identify the viewpoint the text is written form and explore alternatives.

The Lost World

Speaking, listening and drama activities

Objective Use a range of oral techniques to present persuasive arguments and engaging narratives (1.1).

- Ask the children to prepare a speech for the rest of the class, to convince them that the Lost World exists.

Writing activities

Objective In non-narrative, establish, balance and maintain viewpoints (9.3).

- Revisit the features of newspaper reports.
- Discuss the story with the children. What would a news reporter write?
- Design a headline for the story.
- Ask the children to write the news report that Ed Malone might have written on his return from the Lost World.

Assessment *(W, AF2)* Can the children produce news reports that are appropriate to task, reader and purpose?

Whole class reads
Books on a similar theme:
- *Maphead* by Lesley Howarth
- *Journey to the River Sea* by Eva Ibbotson
- *Dinosaur in Danger* by Paul Geraghty
- *Dragonology* by Dugald Steer et al

Cross-curricular links

Science
- Research different types of dinosaurs, looking at habitat, eating habits and food chains.

History
- Explore Aztecs and Incas and other civilizations in South America.

I.C.T./Design & Technology
- Make stop frame animation movies of the Lost World dinosaurs using modelling clay and/or toy figures.

David Copperfield

Author: Charles Dickens (1812–1870)

Synopsis: David Copperfield lives with his mother and their housekeeper, Peggotty. When David's mother marries a very cruel man, Mr Murdstone, David is sent away to Salem House, a run-down London boarding school where he makes friends with a rich boy called Steerforth. David's mother gives birth to a son but sadly, she and the child later die. David is sent away to work at a warehouse by Mr Murdstone. David runs away and lives with his great aunt, Miss Betsey Trotwood, where he has a happier life. David goes to work at a law firm where he meets Uriah Heep, who causes many problems, and Agnes, who becomes a good friend. David resolves the problems caused by Heep and marries a beautiful young woman. Sadly, she dies and David travels, receiving comfort from the letters of his dear friend Agnes. Eventually David returns, becomes a successful writer and marries Agnes.

Social and historical context: The story is set in early Victorian England against a backdrop of great social change. The Industrial Revolution had transformed the social structure of the country and the gap between the rich and poor increased. People moved to cities in search of opportunities and endured poverty and dirty, crowded living conditions. Many children were forced to work long hours.

C = Language comprehension   *R, AF* = Reading Assessment Focus

V = Vocabulary enrichment   *W, AF* = Writing Assessment Focus

Group or guided reading

Introducing the book

(C) *(Predicting)* Ask the children to make predictions about what the story might be about using the front cover and chapter headings. Encourage them to explain why they think something might happen.

(C) *(Clarifying)* Develop the children's understanding of the period by showing pictures from Victorian times and reading extracts that describe schools, Victorian London, family life, and so on.

(V) Display a picture of a Victorian London scene and ask the children to annotate the picture with interesting vocabulary and descriptions of the scene.

During reading

Objective Sustain engagement with longer texts, using different techniques to make the text come alive (8.2).

(C) *(Deducing)* Read Chapters 1–4 with the children. Ask them to consider what sort of life David has had. Show children how to make an emotions graph of the story so far by writing the chapters along the X-axis and different emotions on the Y-axis. Work together to consider David's emotions for the first four chapters.

Assessment *(R, AF3)* Can the children use clues from the text to draw conclusions about the feelings of the main character?

Independent reading

(C) *(Questioning, Clarifying)* Whilst they are reading, ask the children to make notes of any questions that they might like to ask David. They could record these in a reading journal.

- Explore how the Victorian setting influences the storyline and what happens to David.
- Ask the children to complete the emotions graph for the rest of the chapters.

Assessment Check that children:

- *(R, AF3)* can deduce the feelings of the characters in the story
- *(R, AF7)* can identify how the social and historical context influences the characters and the storyline.
- Ask the children to finish reading to the end of the story independently.

Returning and responding to the text

(C) *(Deducing, Summarising)* Focus on the children's emotions graphs and ask: *How have David's emotions changed during the story? What events have had the most impact on him?*

(C) *(Questioning, Imagining)* Ask one of the children to go into role as David Copperfield. Encourage other children to generate questions to ask David.

Assessment Check that children:

- *(R, AF2)* can retrieve and summarise key information from the text
- *(R, AF3)* can deduce, infer and interpret characters' emotions using evidence from the text.

Speaking, listening and drama activities

Objective Use the techniques of dialogic talk to explore, ideas, topics or issues (1.3).

- Invite the children to prepare a brief oral presentation on what life was like for children in Victorian London. Encourage them to use visual aids to add interest.

Writing activities

Objective Select words and language drawing on their knowledge of literary features and formal and informal writing (9.4).

- Briefly remind the children that David Copperfield became a writer.
- Ask the children to recall his life.
- Focus on diary writing and look at examples of diaries, e.g. *The Diary of Anne Frank*.
- Challenge the children to write the events of David's life as a diary extract. Encourage them to try and adopt language from the Victorian era.

Assessment Check that children:

- *(W, AF1)* can put themselves into the mind of David and write imaginative, interesting and thoughtful texts
- *(W, AF7)* can select appropriate and effective vocabulary.

Whole class reads
Books on a similar theme:
- *Oliver Twist* by Charles Dickens
- *The Diary of Anne Frank* by Anne Frank
- *Street Child* by Berlie Doherty
- *Fair's Fair* by Leon Garfield

Cross-curricular links
History
- Study rich and poor communities in Victorian England. You could focus on Victorian schooling and the lives of children.

Art
- Research Victorian cartoons that depict poverty in London. A good place to start is www.cartoonstock.com. Click on 'Vintage Cartoons' to search for 19th century cartoons.

I.C.T.
- Present the diary extracts from the writing activities section as multi-layered I.C.T. texts with hyperlinks to images and sounds.

Moonfleet

Author: John Meade Falkner (1858–1932)

Synopsis: The story tells of the journey and adventures of a 15-year-old orphan boy named John Trenchard. He forms a deep friendship with the local pub landlord, Elzevir Block, who has recently lost his own son at the hands of the local magistrate, Maskew. John and Elzevir go on a journey to find a diamond belonging to Blackbeard and are unfairly imprisoned for ten years, before returning home. They arrive during a storm and Elzevir saves John from drowning, but loses his own life. It is an emotional journey as John learns about himself and develops his own moral stance about life and people.

Social and historical context: The story is set in Dorset in 1757, a time when there was great poverty throughout Britain. The town of Moonfleet is a coastal town and smuggling provides an essential additional income for the residents. It is a tale of morality in which the local vicar sympathises with the impoverished smugglers. The story also explores the emotions of John as he discovers the importance of love and friendship and comes to learn that little good comes from greed. At the end of the story we learn that John has become wealthy, but he has used all his money to build homes for the poor.

C = Language comprehension *R, AF* = Reading Assessment Focus
V = Vocabulary enrichment *W, AF* = Writing Assessment Focus

Group or guided reading

Introducing the book

C *(Predicting)* Look at the front cover and ask the children how the lamp and the diamond might be connected. Ask them to predict what the story might be about.

- Give children the following artefacts: a candle, a fake diamond, a locket, a piece of paper with a few bible verses written on it and toy handcuffs. Discuss with the children how these items might be linked and what importance they might have to the story.

- Take a 'picture walk' through the story. Discuss the illustrations in the book with the children and talk about what the storyline might be.

During reading

Objective Sustain engagement with longer texts, using different techniques to make the text come alive (8.2).

C *(Imagining)* Read Chapters 1–3 with the children. Re-read the beginning of Chapter 1 and ask the children to close their eyes and imagine the scene that John imagines: the ship tossing, the men shouting, etc. Challenge them to create sound effects using their voices and body parts.

C *(Deducing)* Ask the children why they think it is not safe to 'speak your mind' in Moonfleet. What do the children think has happened to John's parents?

Assessment *(R, AF3)* Can the children use clues from the text to draw conclusions?

Independent reading

V Ask the children to read Chapters 4–5. As they are reading ask them to be word detectives and collect vocabulary that is unusual or interesting. They could also include technical language. Invite them to write their words on an appropriately shaped piece of paper, e.g. a ship or diamond shape, and then create a class display.

C *(Clarifying)* Ask the children to consider how John's emotions change during these two chapters.

Assessment Check that children:

- *(R, AF3)* can deduce the main character's emotions from what is said or not said
- *(R, AF5)* understand why the writer has used certain vocabulary in the story.
- Ask the children to finish reading to the end of the story independently.

Returning and responding to the text

C *(Imagining)* Ask the children to create a map of Moonfleet, using evidence from the text to decide what is in the village and its location, e.g. churchyard close to the sea, the *Why Not?* Inn, John's aunt's cottage, the magistrate's Manor house, etc.

C *(Questioning)* Ask the children to think of questions using: Who? What? When? Where? How?

C *(Summarising)* Invite the children to work in pairs to come up with one key sentence to summarise each of the chapters of the story.

Assessment *(R, AF2)* Can the children sum up the key ideas using evidence from the text?

Moonfleet

Speaking, listening and drama activities

Objective Consider the overall impact of a live performance, identifying dramatic ways of conveying characters' ideas and building tension (4.3).

- Ask the children to use drama techniques to recreate the scenes from Chapter 8, from when John and Elzevir arrive at the coast of Moonfleet up to the point when Grace comes to see John. Remind the children to consider how they will convey the characters' emotions and how to build up the tension of the events in their performance.

- Afterwards, discuss the effectiveness of the children's drama presentation. Which techniques were particularly successful?

Writing activities

Objective Select words and language drawing on their knowledge of literary features (9.4).

- Revisit Chapter 1 in which John helps to carve the poem for David's tombstone.

- Talk about Elzevir and his characteristics. Discuss the important events in his life, e.g. loss of his son, befriending John, losing his home to Maskew, giving his life for John, etc.

- Share examples of epitaphs and different poetic forms with the children.

- Ask them to write a poem that could be an epitaph for Elzevir.

Assessment *(W, AF1)* Can the children write original pieces using a range of stylistic features?

Whole class reads
Books on a similar theme:

- *Treasure Island* by Robert Louis Stevenson
- *Plundering Paradise* by Geraldine McCaughrean

Cross-curricular links
Mathematics
- Review imperial measurements and their metric equivalents with the children.

Geography
- Engage the children in mapping the village of Moonfleet and tracking the journey of the two main characters.

Art
- Choose dramatic sections from the story to reproduce as comic strips. For example, illustrate a storyboard from when John hears about Blackbeard's diamond through to when he finds his coffin.